Athletics—Field Events

an Illustrated
Teach Yourself Book

Mike Winch

Tom McNab

Illustrated Teach Yourself

Athletics –
Field Events

**Knight
Books**

ISBN 0 340 19379 4

This edition published 1975 by Knight Books, the
paperback division of Brockhampton Press Ltd, Leicester.
First published in 1972 by Brockhampton Press Ltd
Text copyright © 1972, 1974 Tom McNab
Line drawings copyright © 1972, 1974 Brockhampton Press Ltd
Photographs copyright © 1972 Mark Shearman
Photographs copyright © 1974 Mark Shearman, E.D. Lacey,
Tony Duffy and Tom McNab

Printed in Great Britain by Fletcher & Son Ltd, Norwich.

Contents

To my father

The amazing Wilson

Introduction

In the introduction to ITY ATHLETICS : TRACK EVENTS I described how the exploits of William Wilson, a 150-year-old character from a boys' comic paper, had fired me with enthusiasm for athletics and how, after early failures, I had found a measure of success in triple jump.

My 45′ 11¾″ jump had placed me second in the 1952 British Junior rankings and first in the Scottish Senior rankings for that year. In September 1952, I joined the Royal Air Force to begin two years' National Service. This period produced the first crisis in my athletics career. Up till then I had established no pattern or rhythm of training and the RAF mixture of drill, officer-cadet training and service spit-and-polish, combined with stodgy service food, brought me into 1953 at a lardy 182 lb, 14 lb above my 1952 competitive weight.

The 1953 season was disastrous, with 43′ 6″ as my best distance. I was bewildered. Before that improvements had arrived regularly every year, like Christmas, and I had no idea of what to do to gain my former distances. I ransacked local libraries for books on triple jump but none gave me more than perfunctory information.

By the winter of 1953, I was prepared to give up the sport and to lapse into fatness and lethargy (this at the ripe age of nineteen!) when I received a most surprising letter. It was from the Scottish Empire Games Council and it informed me that I was a 'possible' for the Games which were to be held in Vancouver in the summer of 1954.

This letter spurred me to immediate action. I donned running-gear and plodded off into the winter night. Ten minutes and not much more than a mile later I collapsed on to the floor of my room, my body one great throbbing pulse. Those first days of training were terrible, but after a couple of months I was able to jog three miles without too much distress and in the spring of 1954 I went on a Fighter Command Athletics Training Course feeling that I was fit enough to take whatever punishment was meted out to me.

I was wrong. After three-quarters of an hour of warming-up I was back again to the 'throbbing pulse' of two months before. Luckily, rain intervened and we were ushered into a lecture-room to see a film. This, I thought, would be a good opportunity to hide, to sleep, to recover. Surprisingly, it was none of these things. Rather a major turning-point in my athletics life, a point at which I was to decide whether or not I was to remain a dilettante, or to become a true athlete.

The film was *Olympiad, Festival of Nations* by Leni Riefenstahl on the 1936 Olympics. Riefenstahl represented the athlete as a hero, triumphing over all challenges, even in failure. The final sequences, showing marathon runners who had lost all hopes of victory doggedly stumbling towards the stadium, determined to finish at all costs, are one of the great film-sequences of all time and there were more than a few nose-blowings and coughs when the lights went on.

This was it! If this was what athletics was about, the challenge of defeating time, height and distance and in the end defeating yourself, then this was for me. From that moment, my fate was sealed. I went on that season to take the Scottish triple jump title with $47'7\frac{1}{2}''$, to rank second in the British Senior rankings (albeit a poor second) and to fail narrowly to make the Scottish Empire Games team.

More important, I went on to compete for another eight years in athletics in sprints, jumps, throws and decathlon. Looking back, I would do the same again, only better, because now I have the advantage of knowing how to prepare myself physically and psychologically for athletics competition.

I have described how a comic-paper character and an Olympics film provided me with the motivation to pursue what turned out to be an exciting and enjoyable athletics career. This book will, I hope, provide a similar spur to your athletics activity. I did, however, say that even with this motivation my training tended to be haphazard, because I could find no guidance in athletics books. This book is an attempt to give crisp, simple guidance to you in an easily-assimilated form.

Remember that athletics is a series of diverse physical tests, the field events being tests of skill and power. The 'fun' is in preparing yourself to meet these challenges and in the golden moments when the shot breaks new turf, your heels cut fresh sand and when the inside of your thigh sweeps round a cross-bar that has always previously fallen to the ground.

The National Sports Centre, Crystal Palace

General

Is it necessary to join a club?

Since the club is the basic competitive unit, there are few ways of competing in track and field athletics (apart from rare 'open' meetings) other than by being a member of a club. This apart, the club offers great advantages in terms of coaching, fellowship and facilities.

How do I know which club is the best one to join?

In some areas you will have no choice! In other more densely-populated areas there may be several clubs from which to choose. It is best to move towards a club which has an active youth section. If a club has officials who are interested in young people, then it is investing in success. Check with your physical education teacher and he will be able to advise you.

Can I join two clubs?

Yes, but you are 'first claim' to the club which you first join. This means that your first club always has prior claim on your services. It also means that although you can compete for any number of 'second-claim' clubs in minor two-club meetings, you *cannot* compete for a 'second-claim' club in major meetings involving three or more clubs, such as League or Trophy meetings.

What need is there for this 'first-claim' rule?

Club secretaries are only human, and if no such rule existed, athletes would be enticed away from their 'first-claim' clubs to compete for other clubs. Thus no club would be able to rely on a 'core' of regular competitors.

What if an athlete moves to another area?

An application to his Area Association will usually enable him immediately to join a new club without having to wait the normal nine months required before changing clubs. Also, if an athlete is, say, a walker and his club ceases to cater for walking, an application to his Area Association will usually enable him to change to a more suitable club.

Moment of victory. Mary Peters on the victory rostrum in Munich

If I attend a University or College, who has 'first claim' upon me?

Your College or University has 'first claim' upon you during your period of study. The same applies while you are *at school*, in that your school also has 'first claim' upon you.

Does the school having claims ahead of your athletics club present problems?

It certainly does! Many clubs feel that, since they offer a young athlete the most in terms of quality of coaching and competition, they rather than the school have been the main factor in his development and should have first claim on his services. This problem frequently turns up during the cross-country season when the school wants a boy in the morning for soccer and the club wishes him (in good condition!) for an afternoon cross-country race. My feeling is that when an inter-sport tug of war takes place, the boy should have the final choice. On the other hand, when the 'battle' concerns whether or not an athlete should *run* for school or club, then the school should have first claim.

What are the fees for being a member of a club?

These are usually on a sliding scale, the youngest members paying least and the eldest most. The range might be:

13-15   25p-50p per annum
15-17   25p-75p per annum
17-19   50p-£1.50 per annum

Most clubs usually also have a nightly track fee, payable to the local authority, of about 5p.

What competition is available in clubs?

1. The internal club championship.
2. Friendly matches with other clubs.
3. Trophy matches.
4. League matches.

Trophy matches are usually annual 4-6 club affairs for a cup or shield. They offer an excellent type of competition. League matches are of two types, regional and national, for men only. Every English region has leagues, divided into divisions. The top clubs of the regional leagues meet at the end of the season for two places in the fourth division of the national league. The national league has four divisions of six teams, with two teams promoted and two relegated from each division. This league competition is the highest level of competition which club track and field athletics offer. In 1972, a national knock-out cup was instituted, so athletics now has a wide range of competitive incentives.

The author with one of his athletes, long jumper Maureen Chitty

Is a coach essential?

Many athletes have reached world-class performances with little coaching. This particularly applies to middle-distance and long-distance runners, who are not beset with the technical problems of field events' athletes. It is probably true to say that it is now impossible to reach world-class in field events without coaching. However, 99% of those who read this book will never reach such high levels of performance. This does not mean that they do not need help. I would, however, stress that it is possible to reach surprisingly high levels of performance using the eyes of a friend and your own personal sensations as your guide.

What do you mean by 'personal sensations'?

I mean the feed-back you get from your muscles whenever you perform any movement. You must teach yourself to be sensitive to these muscular sensations and to other types of feed-back such as those which you get from your eyes and from a friend who may be able to pick out errors which you yourself may not have sensed.

How important is warm-up?

Very important. Warm-up gets you ready physically, by raising muscle-temperature and increasing blood-supply to the muscles, and mentally by getting you into that slightly 'jittery' condition essential to good performance. I would, however, stress that the warm-up for a middle-distance run is quite different from that for an explosive event like long jump. A middle-distance warm-up might consist of a mile jog and half a dozen strides down the straight. A long jump warm-up might be 800 metres jogging, some stretching exercises, some sprints and some approach-run practices.

How important is a good technique?

Technique is freedom. By that I mean that a good technique provides you with a framework within which you can express your strength and suppleness effectively. The danger, however, is getting bogged down in technical detail. The first thing with any event is to decide what is important and what is not. There will at any one time be only two or three important technical factors. If you push these hard, then you are well on your way to success.

Do I require any special diet?

Any diet should be composed of carbohydrates, fats and proteins. Carbohydrates and fats are necessary for the production of immediate energy and protein is essential for growth. Protein can be taken as meat, milk or fish.

What about pre-competition meals?

Here protein is of little value as it cannot release immediate energy. Another problem is bulk and digestion-time, for competing after a heavy meal which the stomach is still digesting can be uncomfortable. A light, easily-digested carbohydrate meal, supplemented by a glucose drink such as 'Dynamo', is best.

What do you advise on strength-training?

Strength is essential in all 'power-events' and even to some extent in middle-distance running. Try to set yourself a definite programme, working on the basis of lifting each weight 8–10 times, this constituting a 'set'. A programme might consist of :

    a: 3 sets of 10 light dumbell repetitions (arm or leg exercise)
    b: 3 sets of 8 repetitions (arm exercise)
    c: 3 sets of 8 repetitions (leg exercise)
    d: 3 sets of 10 repetitions (abdominal exercise)
With exercises (*b*) and (*c*) a relatively heavy weight must be used.

Is there any reason for this particular sequence of exercise?
    Yes. The relatively light arm exercise (*b*) is placed early in the
programme at a time when you are fresh. If you placed a heavy, sapping
leg exercise before the arm exercise, you would find it difficult to produce
good quality work in the arm exercise. Exercises (*a*) and (*d*) are 'warm-up'
and 'cool-down' exercises.

This session seems much lighter than those in athletics magazines.
    It is. It relates to the needs of a young person who may only have 20–30
minutes during lunch-break to perform his weight-training and with only
limited equipment. A simple, crisp, easily performed session is more
realistic than an advanced one which might simply deter you from even
beginning weight-training!

Do I need to work with other athletes during my weight-training?
    Yes, if only for safety. A second reason is that friends help to
provide 'atmosphere' and motivate you to harder work.

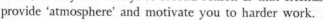

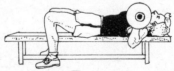

Bench press (heavy weight training – arm exercise)

Dumbell curl (light weight training
– warm-up exercise)

Power clean (heavy weight training – leg exercise)

Squat (heavy weight training — leg exercise)

Leg lift (light weight training — abdominal exercise)

What about suppling exercises?

These are essential. Naturally, the more specialised you become the more specific these exercises must be. Every session should contain a sequence of suppling exercises. You must be loose and elastic.

Leg swings (suppling exercise)

Trunk circling (suppling exercise)

The Russian 'flopper' Shapka, 1971 European Games Gold Medallist

High Jump

Height in high-jump heights is measured perpendicularly from the ground to the lowest point of the cross-bar. A competitor fails if he:

1. Dislodges the bar from its pegs.
2. Touches the landing-area beyond the plane of the uprights without first clearing the bar.
3. Takes off from both feet.

Ties are decided as follows:

In jumping or vaulting for height:

1. The competitor with the lowest number of jumps at the height *at which the tie occurs* shall be awarded the higher place.
2. If the tie still remains, the competitor with the lowest total of failures throughout the competition up to and including the height last cleared shall be awarded the higher place.

3. If the tie still remains, the competitor with the lowest total number of jumps (whether successful or not) throughout the competition up to and including the height last cleared shall be awarded the higher place.

EXAMPLE :

High Jump

	5'6" 1.67m	5'8" 1.72m	5'9" 1.75m	5'10" 1.77m	5'11" 1.80m	6'0" 1.82m	6'1" 1.85m	Total Failures	Total Jumps	Position
Jones	−	x/	/	x/	−	xx/	*All*	4	8	2
Smith	/	/	/	x	x/	xx/	*failed*	4	9	3
Brown	/	/	x	/	xx/	xx/	*three*	5	10	4
Black	/ ·	−	−	xx/	xx/	x/	*times*	5	9	1

The 'failures' rule seems complicated.
It is rarely carried to its limits. If you take the minimum number of jumps and make plenty of first-attempt clearances, it need never worry you. Note that Black gains first place because he cleared 6'0" on his second attempt. Jones gains second place because, though he has the same number of failures as Smith, he has had fewer jumps. Smith gains third place on fewer failures than Brown.

What happens if you clear the bar, but touch it and it falls to the ground after you have moved away from the landing-area?
This would count as a 'foul'. If you have knocked the bar down it is a 'foul', no matter how long it takes to fall. But in a high wind the judge may decide that the wind may be the main reason for the bar falling and the jump may not be ruled a 'foul'.

High jump seems to be less 'natural' than long jump.
True. The technique of the approach-run and take-off is completely artificial, in contrast to the relatively 'natural' uninhibited sprinting of the long-jump approach and take-off. Both long and high jump have artificial flight-techniques, but on balance high jump is the less 'natural' of the two jumps.

A basic Scissors. Note the amount of body weight which has to be lifted above bar level in order to clear the lowest part of the body

Ann Wilson performs a crisp, neat Western Roll. Compare this compact, economic technique with the Scissors above

The Straddle. Note how the body lies *along* the bar

The Fosbury Flop.
Dick Fosbury arches his way
to victory in Mexico.
The Flop has enabled many young
jumpers to clear remarkable heights.
Its great asset is its simplicity

Does 'flight-technique' mean techniques such as Western Roll, Straddle and Fosbury Flop?

Yes. The high-jumper works against gravity and his first problem is to raise his centre of gravity as high as possible at take-off. Once he is in the air, he can clear higher cross-bars only by disposing his body differently around the bar.

So the various techniques don't give you any more 'lift' in mid-air?

Correct. There is no means of propelling yourself while in mid-air, short of strapping a rocket to your back! What the jumper does is *to avoid the bar* by getting into more economic positions. The 'Scissors' is the least economic, because there is a great deal of mass above the centre of gravity, and the 'Straddle' and 'Fosbury' the most economic.

Is the 'Fosbury Flop' worth considering?

Yes. I shall deal with this technique later. However many British landing-areas are simply not yet up to the demands of the 'Flop'. Naturally a safe landing-area is essential for this technique.

How important is a good flight-technique?

It is considerably less important than a good approach-run and take-off. It is in the approach-run and at take-off that the big leaps are made.

What are the priorities in approach-run?

First, accuracy! Let us assume that you are performing a Straddle from the left foot. Stand side-on to the bar and reach out. Then run away from

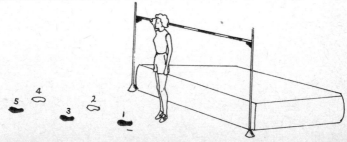

the bar at about 35°–40°, checking the fifth stride. Then run back from this point and jump, landing on your right leg.

Have you any other points?

Several. Try to keep the trunk upright at take-off. It is UP FIRST, LAY-OUT LAST! Try also to drop the right arm and shoulder down when you are at bar level.

What about the trail-leg?

Keep this leg folded and rotate it *round the bar*. Make no attempt to lift it or straighten it.

Most Straddle jumpers seem to land on their backs.

Yes, but if you try to do this in the early stages, at low heights, you will tend to 'dive' rather than jump. *Take-off lift must never be sacrificed to flight-technique.* As you reach greater heights you will find that you have more time to rotate and will tend to land on your right shoulder and upper back.

Is the extra speed from, say, an 8-stride approach-run of value?

Initially, speed is an enemy. When, however, you have achieved a solid, stable approach-run and take-off, then a little extra speed can be of value.

What are the basics of the approach-run?

First, accuracy, which we have already dealt with. Next, an upright trunk at take-off, essential if you are going to get good lift. It is useful to plant a corner-flag in the landing-area, in line with your approach-run, and to keep your eyes on it till the last moment. This will help keep you upright.

Ann Hull shows an excellent free-leg swing

This I understand. What about the type of running – I have been told that I should have a bouncy, springy approach-run.

This is not so. The type of running in the first couple of strides is not too important. What *is* important is the last three strides. These must be *flat-footed*, with bent knees. A good idea is to put a check-mark three strides out. When you hit this mark, get on to your heels.

Are there any other points about these last few strides?

They must be long. When you hit your check-mark think of long – l - o - n - g - e - r – leap!

Is the last stride the longest?

No. The penultimate (last but one) is the longest. This is where the big 'settle' takes place.

Should these last three strides be fast?

Not for the beginner. The feeling should be of holding speed through these strides. Keep pressing the hips forward in these 'settling' strides.

Have you any other points?

Make sure that you run in a straight line all the way in to the bar. One way of ensuring this is to scrape a line from the start of your run to take-off. And try to *swing* at the bar with your free leg. The main point is to think in terms of *leap first* and lay-out last!

The Fosbury Flop

Have many young jumpers made big improvements using the Fosbury Flop?

Yes. For the jumper who has limited time or is having great difficulties with the Straddle, the Flop is ideal. Indeed, I am coming round to the view that the Flop is best for about 80% of young jumpers.

What about the danger of back injuries?

There is no hard evidence that if safe, commercially made landing-areas are used the Flop is any more dangerous than the Straddle.

What, then, are the basics?

First, try a 'Scissors' jump from a 5-stride approach. Next, do the same, dropping back in mid-air so that you land on your back.

What is the reason for these practices?

To give you the 'feel' of scissoring to land on your back safely. 'Fosbury' is, after all, just that, a back lay-out scissors. Now scrape out a semi-circular curve on the approach-run from the middle of the bar, and again stride out your 5-stride approach-run. Run in and jump.

Will I be able to 'Flop' immediately from this new curved run?

Probably not. You will almost certainly simply sail through the air in a hunched-up position at a slight angle to the bar, like a flying sack of potatoes! Still, try this a few times, even if it is a crude leap, just to get the sensation of running in smoothly from a curved run.

What next?

Jump high and try to turn so that you are at right-angles to the bar. Think in terms of driving up and sweeping the lead knee up and across your body. You may still be quite bunched up going over the bar, but you will have the basic jump and turn.

More and more schools and clubs are buying the safe landing areas essential for the Fosbury Flop

How do I achieve the flat 'Fosbury' position?

First, try jumping from the spot, throwing your hips forward as in a standing long jump, to get the 'feel' of the extended position. Now try running in from your curved run, thinking of SPRING AND HIP-FLIP! It is this flip-up of the hips which gives you your flat lay-out on the bar.

What other advice do you give?

If you find that the hip-flip does not produce the required lay-out, try dropping the shoulders back at the peak of your flight.

When I increase my speed, does this mean an increase in approach-run distance?

Yes, but the run must flatten out in the first strides, curving in only over the last 3–4 strides. This means, in fact, that on your longer approach-runs you approach at a *tangent* to the bar.

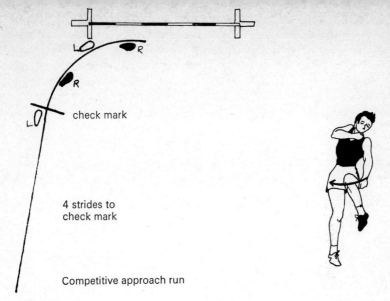

check mark

4 strides to
check mark

Competitive approach run

Should I have a check-mark at this curve-in point?
   Yes. Otherwise your approach-run will tend to be erratic.

What about the rear-leg action?
   Think of dangling both legs behind you, of 'kicking yourself' with your heels.

What is the action after bar-clearance?
   'Give' quickly at the hips and flip the lower legs upwards.

Surely the flop is dangerous when you land on the bar?
   Yes, this is why you should always use rounded fibre-glass bars, or even elasticated bars for training purposes.

What about a special shoe for the take-off foot?
   This is not important until you are a committed jumper but a built-up shoe with heel spikes is essential at this level. A photograph of a take-off shoe is shown below.

High Jump: Boys scoring tables

Amount per extra point   1″/0.025m

35 points	5′ 10″	– 1.77
34	5′ 9″	– 1.75
33	5′ 8″	– 1.72
32	5′ 7″	– 1.70
31	5′ 6″	– 1.67
30	5′ 5″	– 1.65
29	5′ 4″	– 1.62
28	5′ 3″	– 1.60
27	5′ 2″	– 1.57
26	5′ 1″	– 1.55
25	5′ 0″	– 1.52
24	4′ 11″	– 1.50
23	4′ 10″	– 1.47
22	4′ 9″	– 1.45
21	4′ 8″	– 1.42
20	4′ 7″	– 1.39
19	4′ $5\frac{1}{2}$″	– 1.36
18	4′ $4\frac{1}{2}$″	– 1.33
17	4′ 3″	– 1.29
16	4′ 2″	– 1.26
15	4′ 0″	– 1.22
14	3′ 11″	– 1.19
13	3′ $9\frac{1}{2}$″	– 1.15
12	3′ 8″	– 1.12
11	3′ $6\frac{1}{2}$″	– 1.08
10	3′ $5\frac{1}{2}$″	– 1.05
9	3′ 4″	– 1.01·
8	3′ $2\frac{1}{2}$″	– 0.98
7	3′ 1″	– 0.94
6	3′ 0″	– 0.91
5	2′ $10\frac{1}{2}$″	– 0.87
4	2′ 9″	– 0.84
3	2′ $7\frac{1}{2}$″	– 0.80
2	2′ $6\frac{1}{2}$″	– 0.77
1	2′ 5″	– 0.73

High Jump: Girls scoring tables

Amount per extra point $\frac{5}{8}''$/0.015m

35 points	5′ 1$\frac{1}{4}$″ − 1.56
34	5′ 1″ − 1.55
33	5′ 0$\frac{1}{4}$″ − 1.53
32	4′ 11$\frac{3}{4}$″ − 1.52
31	4′ 11″ − 1.50
30	4′ 10$\frac{1}{2}$″ − 1.49
29	4′ 9$\frac{3}{4}$″ − 1.47
28	4′ 9$\frac{1}{2}$″ − 1.46
27	4′ 8$\frac{3}{4}$″ − 1 44
26	4′ 8$\frac{1}{4}$″ − 1.43
25	4′ 7$\frac{1}{2}$″ − 1.41
24	4′ 7″ − 1.40
23	4′ 6$\frac{1}{4}$″ − 1.38
22	4′ 6″ − 1.37
21	4′ 5″ − 1.35
20	4′ 4$\frac{3}{4}$″ − 1.34
19	4′ 3$\frac{1}{2}$″ − 1.31
18	4′ 2$\frac{1}{4}$″ − 1.28
17	4′ 0$\frac{3}{4}$″ − 1.24
16	3′ 11$\frac{1}{2}$″ − 1.21
15	3′ 10″ − 1.17
14	3′ 8$\frac{3}{4}$″ − 1.14
13	3′ 7$\frac{1}{4}$″ − 1.10
12	3′ 6″ − 1.07
11	3′ 4$\frac{1}{2}$″ − 1.03
10	3′ 3$\frac{1}{4}$″ − 1.00
9	3′ 1$\frac{3}{4}$″ − 0.96
8	3′ 0$\frac{1}{2}$″ − 0.93
7	2′ 11″ − 0.89
6	2′ 9$\frac{3}{4}$″ − 0.86
5	2′ 8$\frac{1}{4}$″ − 0.82
4	2′ 7″ − 0.79
3	2′ 5$\frac{1}{2}$″ − 0.75
2	2′ 4$\frac{1}{4}$″ − 0.72
1	2′ 3″ − 0.69

British pole vault record-holder Mike Bull

Pole Vault

Some historians say that the event began in the Fens of East Anglia, where countrymen had to clear ditches by using long poles. There is, however, little evidence of this. Modern vaulting began in the middle of the 19th century in Scotland and the Lake District. Scottish immigrants took the event to the United States and the event became fully international in 1900 when it was introduced into the Olympic programme.

The rules are similar to high jump, the main difference being that if a vaulter clears the bar and his pole drops *under* it, this is counted as a clearance. If, however, his pole drifts through and knocks the bar down, then this is a 'foul' vault.

If I run in, plant the pole and make no attempt to take off, is that a 'foul'?

No. It would, however, be a 'foul', first if you attempted to take off and second if you made no attempt to take off but placed your pole on the landing-area beyond the uprights.

Are there two methods of pole-vaulting, one for a steel pole and the other for fibre-glass?

At low level (the 6'–10' range) there is only one method of vaulting and that is the steel-pole technique. This is not to say that many young athletes could not start to use a fibre-glass pole before 10' is cleared. Rather it is because few schools have fibre-glass poles and you will probably have to have cleared around 10' (3.05m) before your teacher will consider it worth buying you one.

What is the advantage of the fibre-glass pole?

The main limitation on the height a vaulter can clear is the height of his top hand on the pole. The fibre-glass pole, because of its flexibility, produces a short fast-moving lever and thus allows you to hold higher. Also, its recoil as it straightens gives you lift off the pole.

I have been told that pole vault is a complicated event.

Any athletics event is complicated if you go into enough detail! Pole vault is initially simply run, plant, hang and swing. Many boys have cleared 13' (3.96m) and above without knowing much more than this.

What is meant by 'plant'?

This is the placing of the pole in the box at take-off.

Are there any practices I can do before I attempt to vault for height?

Several. First, try supported vaulting with a friend.

The rope vault

This simply involves running in off a short run on to the pole, which is held by your friend. Aided by your speed, he lifts the pole to the vertical, swinging you into the landing-area. There are two points here:
1. Stand in direct line with the pole, so that it 'splits' you.
2. Run into the pole, making no attempt to jump on to it.

What other practices are there?

   'Soft' plants involving planting the pole into a long-jump pit is another practice. This reduces the shock of taking off from a hard vaulting box. Rope-vaults are also good preparation.

Alan Williams uses the 'Bantex' beginners' fibre-glass pole

It is essential to have safe landing areas for pole-vaulting

How do I hold the pole?

Think in terms of two Vs. The back V is the right hand, pointing backwards, with a firm grip on the pole. The front V is formed by the thumb supporting (not gripping) the pole. Shoulders are square to the front.

Are these 'plants' into sand for height?

They can be both for height and for distance. The main idea is simply to *hang* on the pole and drift through. Make no attempt to pull or push on the pole.

Surely there is a pull and a push in vaulting?

There is, indeed, but initially you must get used to letting the pole do the work. An early pull slows up the pole.

How far up the pole should I hold?

Most novices can hold in the 9'0" to 10'6" range. Finding the right hand-hold is a matter of trial and error. The best advice is to start with a low hand-hold. If you can raise the pole to the vertical with this low hand-hold, start to inch your hands gradually up the pole until the pole no longer reaches the vertical position during your vault.

How long an approach-run should I take?

Nine strides will do for training, as this will allow you many vaults with minimum fatigue. This will lengthen to 13–19 strides for competition.

Do I keep my hands fixed on the pole?

Initially, yes. When, however, you have got the 'feel' of running and planting into sand, try 'shifting' the bottom hand up to meet the top hand at 'plant'. This helps you to get the pole much higher at take-off and makes for an easier 'hang'.

Any other points?

Keep the pole-tip low at the beginning of your run and *keep it steady* during your run.

When should I move to 'planting' into the vault-box?

As soon as possible! It is best here to work with a friend – indeed it is a good idea to vault with a friend at all times, as a matter of safety. Have your friend stand at the box on your left as you vault. As you plant he will grip the pole and assist it to the vertical position, as in the 'support vault' previously described.

What should I think of at this point?

Think of bowling the pole ahead of you through a loose left hand, sweeping it *in and up* at take-off.

Think, too, of staying behind the pole.

How many vaults should I take before I go on to other points?

Dozens. When you can plant and hang, then the other aspects of the vault, the swing, pull and push are relatively easy to perform.

How long should I continue on supported vaults?

Naturally you will want to vault 'solo' as soon as possible. As soon as you feel capable of vaulting without support, do so.

What about stand-placement?

A good point. The stands should be placed well back at low heights to give you time to execute your vault. As you get higher, the stands should be brought closer in.

And the swing, pull and push?

Here I have found it useful to bring back the supporter, because if the swing is badly timed, the pole often tends to slow up and drop backwards. Your supporter can prevent you from falling back on to hard ground. Put the hands up six inches – this will give you a little more time in the air. 'Hang' long then *tuck fast*, bringing the knees up to the chest. This will bring you above your hand-hold for the first time and lead you into some sort of pushing position.

Should I have a bar up for these vaults?

No. A bar can be a distraction at this point. A good practical point is to use a strip of elastic as a cheap alternative bar.

Are there any other things to think about?

Try to increase your approach-run and inch up your hands on the pole. This will give you more time to 'hang' and swing.

What dictates the height a vaulter can hold on the pole?

1. Running-speed – the faster you can run with the pole (assuming you can 'plant' and take-off effectively) the higher you can hold.
2. The height of the vaulter – even with the same speed, a taller vaulter can hold higher on the pole than a small one, yet only have to put it through the same angle.
3. A smooth, fluent 'plant' and take-off.

Fibre-glass Vaulting

What is the basic difference between steel and fibre-glass vaulting?

Simply, the *bend*! This makes for a higher hand-hold, allowing you to leave the pole at a higher point. The main practical point is that there is no shift of the hands on the pole.

What equipment do I require?

First, make sure that you have a safe landing-area. Built up, well-dug sand is acceptable for steel-vaulting at low heights, as you usually tend to land feet-first. Sand is useless for fibre-glass vaulting as even in the early stages you must land on your back. A serviceable area can be made from bags of foam, preferably covered with a waterproof sheet, but every school or club must aim for a proper commercially-made landing-area.

A good fibre-glass pole, such as the 'Bantex', can be bought for about £25. This is a British pole and goes as low as an 85-lb stress-weight.

Stress-weight?

If you are to achieve a bend, you must have a pole which you are capable of bending. Poles are graded according to weight, a 190-lb pole being the heaviest and an 85-lb the lightest. This means that a vaulter of these weights could hold the pole at maximum height and achieve good bend and recoil without breaking it.

Does this mean that a vaulter must buy a pole directly related to his body-weight?

Initially, no. A 140-lb novice vaulter might require a 120-lb pole in his early learning period as he would find it difficult to bend a 140-lb pole. After he has learnt to bend on the light pole he graduates to the heavier one. It is only when he starts to achieve a high hand-hold and big bends on the light pole that he is in danger of breaking it.

So the idea is to buy a pole below body-weight?

Yes. If you have reached the stage of needing a fibre-glass pole, you should know other vaulters with whom you can exchange your pole when you grow out of it.

Mike Bull

How do I achieve bend?
    First, the shift must vanish. Off a short run, vault, keeping the hands steady on the pole. If you tape the pole at the lower-hand grip you will find it easier to avoid 'shifting'. Some sticky Venice turpentine on both hands will give you a solid grip.

Is the 'plant' different with fibre-glass?
    Yes. Sweep the pole *over-arm* into the box. TRY TO GET THE POLE WELL OUT IN FRONT BEFORE PLANTING. This will give you time to perform your take-off.

Will I have achieved some bend by this time?
    Possibly, but it will probably only be a flicker, rather than a bend. First, you must feel that you can bend the pole. Try 'planting' from a 3-stride walk. Get the left arm directly behind the pole and *drive* forward into the box. This will bend the pole and give you the feel of the pole bellying out in front.

Any other points?

Yes. Try now to vault for distance, keeping the left arm as straight as possible, to keep you away from the pole. You will find the bend beginning to increase.

How can I improve this bend?

When you feel confident, increase your approach-run distance and start to inch up your hands. The greater your speed and the more pole you have in front of you, the greater your potential bend.

How many training sessions will it take me to reach this stage?

This is difficult to say. The danger with a book like this is that skill-learning can seem to be a simple 1–2–3 process. Alas, life is not like that! It may take you a hundred vaults before you can get a reasonable bend. When you do, it will be worth it!

Have you any other pointers?

Try sinking a vault-box into the long-jump pit. This 'deep' box will help you achieve better bends and give you the feel of sinking backwards as the pole moves forwards.

When should I try to clear a bar?

As soon as you feel you are achieving reasonable bend. Otherwise you will simply revert to your old 'steel' technique in order to clear the bar.

Could you summarise the points so far?

1. Wide (12″–18″) hand-spacing.
2. No shift.
3. Early high over-arm plant.
4. Strong left arm behind pole.
5. Keep left arm fixed while in the air, to keep you away from the pole.

Do you have any more advanced points?

Yes. At this stage you are simply planting, bending and dropping over the bar as the pole straightens. You must next attempt to bring up the knees and drop on to your back as the pole bends. This gets your body into a more vertical position relative to the pole, so that when it straightens it lifts you.

Does the pole bend out directly in front of me? How do I know it is not going to bend across me?

An excellent point, if only for self-preservation. Every pole has a 'bend-point', a spot at which it bends best. This the manufacturer usually marks with his trade-mark. If it is not marked, you can find the 'bend-point' by rolling the pole about in your fingers. You will see it begin to sag at one point.

How do I grip the pole so that the bend-point is correctly placed at take-off?

Hold the pole so that the bend-point is at around '3 o'clock'. As the pole revolves at 'plant' it will turn to '10 o'clock'.

Do you have any other advice?

Yes. In taking up vaulting, you are competing in what is possibly the most challenging of all field events. In it you will meet the cream of athletes. Make sure you do yourself justice by working hard to master pole-vaulting, the skill of the brave.

Pole Vault: Boys scoring tables

Amount per extra point   4"/0.10m

35 points	11′ 3¾″ − 3.45
34	11′ 0″ − 3.35
33	10′ 8″ − 3.25
32	10′ 4″ − 3.15
31	10′ 0″ − 3.05
30	9′ 8¼″ − 2.95
29	9′ 4¼″ − 2.85
28	9′ 0¼″ − 2.75
27	8′ 8¼″ − 2.65
26	8′ 4½″ − 2.55
25	8′ 0½″ − 2.45
24	7′ 10½″ − 2.40
23	7′ 8½″ − 2.35
22	7′ 6½″ − 2.30
21	7′ 4½″ − 2.25
20	7′ 2¾″ − 2.20
19	7′ 0¾″ − 2.15
18	6′ 10¾″ − 2.10
17	6′ 8¾″ − 2.05
16	6′ 6¾″ − 2.00
15	6′ 4¾″ − 1.95
14	6′ 2¾″ − 1.90
13	6′ 0¾″ − 1.85
12	5′ 11″ − 1.80
11	5′ 9″ − 1.75
10	5′ 7″ − 1.70
9	5′ 5″ − 1.65
8	5′ 3″ − 1.60
7	5′ 1″ − 1.55
6	4′ 11″ − 1.50
5	4′ 9″ − 1.45
4	4′ 7¼″ − 1.40
3	4′ 5¼″ − 1.35
2	4′ 3¼″ − 1.30
1	4′ 1¼″ − 1.25

Olympic gold-medallist Heidi Rosendahl

Long Jump

Distances are measured from the furthest back point of landing to the
nearest edge of the take-off board. 'Fouling' occurs if the jumper
over-steps the board or runs past the plane of the board, even if he makes
no attempt to jump. Normally 3–6 attempts are allowed each jumper.
If there is a 'tie' then the jumper with the next best jump wins.

Is long jump the most 'natural' of the jumping events?

Yes. The technical factors in long jump are much fewer and less complex than in the other three jumps. Several schoolboys have leapt 23' (7.01m) in long jump without training, but one rarely sees an untrained schoolboy vault 13'0" (3.96m) or triple jump 48'0" (14.63m).

What are the technical essentials?

Long jump is simply a fast, accurate run flowing into a high jump. The first essential is therefore an accurate approach-run.

How long should the approach-run be?

The length is related to basic speed. A girl of twelve capable of running 100 metres in 14 seconds might require an approach-run of only 13 strides, while an eighteen-year-old capable of 12 seconds might require a 19-stride approach.

How do I secure an approach-run?

There are two ways. One is to ask a friend to check the distance you cover in a certain number of strides. Run this through in the same direction as the long-jump approach-run, making six attempts, so that you can achieve some level of consistency. Then try to place this approach-run on the long-jump run-way and make some attempts to jump. Ask your friend to check each *second* stride – this makes it easier to count.

The other method is to stand on the take-off board and run back a certain number of strides, asking a friend to check on your final foot-mark. Starting from this mark, you run back towards the board and jump.

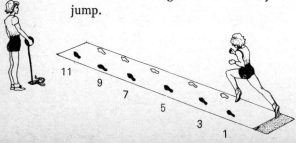

What are the advantages and disadvantages of each method?

Method 2 is effective in still conditions. If, however, there is a following or a retarding wind, the run away from the board and the run back towards it will not match.

The first method is more likely to produce an approach-run which will 'match' when placed on the run-way, because it relates to whatever wind or slope conditions prevail.

I have been told that a good long-jumper can hit the board blindfold. Is this true?

No, not really. Any approach-run involves two factors, one being the reproduction of fast fluent running and the other the ability to adjust one's running *during the approach-run itself*. No two approach-runs are exactly the same, so the 'blindfold' idea will not stand up to investigation. Any good jumper has to make adjustments on every stride from start to finish of the run.

Should the eyes be focused on the board?

No. You must be *aware* of the board but must not keep your eyes pinned to it. Otherwise, there is a tendency for the head to be down, making it difficult for you to get up off the board.

Should I try to run faster in the last few strides before take-off?

No, but there must be no 'coasting' or slackening off in these strides. Try to keep running strongly into the board.

Should I use check-marks on the approach-run?

You are not *allowed* to mark, or place markers on, the run-way. Any markers must be placed *alongside* it. I suggest only one check-mark, early (5–7 strides from the start) in your approach-run. If your check-mark is too close to the board, you have insufficient time to make adjustments and it will in any case take your mind off hard strong running in the last strides before take-off.

I have been told that I should 'run off the board' at take-off. Is this right?

No. The take-off is a definite 'strike'. There must be sufficient contact to give you upward lift. Your aim must be to 'strike' on and off the board. This is not a stamping action, but a drive up and away from the board.

Should the body be upright at take-off?

It *must* be! If your approach-run is over-short, there is a danger that your trunk will not be sufficiently upright at take-off, but with the correct approach-run length you should be sufficiently upright.

British long jump record holder, Lynn Davies, hitch-kicks in a training leap

Are there any other factors at take-off?

Yes. In your short, practice approach-runs (5–11 strides) stress

1. 'Strike' off the board.
2. Extending the take-off leg off the board. Feel that you have squeezed everything from the leg muscles before taking them from the board.
3. High thigh and chest.

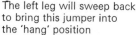

The left leg will sweep back
to bring this jumper into
the 'hang' position

Good take-off extension and
high free knee.
Nothing to spare on the board

What of technique in the air?

For beginners, this is the least important factor, the priorities being
plenty of hard, accurate running and explosive leaping. If you can do this,
you have gone 90% of the way to jumping well.

The first aim is a deceptively simple one, simply to practise landing
with *heels parallel to the board*. Even good-class jumpers often land with
the heels out of line. Since distance is measured from the furthest point
back, this is sheer carelessness.

Bob Beamon (U.S.A.) jumps into history with his Mexico leap of 8·9 metres

Is the hitch-kick of value?

Not unless you are clearing a fair distance, certainly above 18′0″ (5.48m). Otherwise, the gains are negligible. The real danger is that in concentrating on a flight-technique like hitch-kick you spoil the essentials of approach-run speed and lift. Still, some form of flight-technique can be of value. The 'hang', used by many top athletes, is simple to learn.

Maureen Chitty, 1972 WAAA Indoor long jump champion. Note the excellent erect trunk

What advantage does such a technique give the jumper?
  It helps him to get his feet further out on landing.

What is the best method of learning the 'hang'?
Try a few standing long jumps into the pit.

This will give the 'feel' of the 'hang' position. Next, using a 'beat' board, and a short (5–7 stride) approach jump into the pit, land in a 'splits' position.

Try this a few times. Last, sweep the lead leg out and back and this will put you into the majestic 'hang' position.

When do I leave out the beat-board?

As soon as you feel that you can handle the 'hang' from the ground. Remember to stress getting *up first*, before 'hanging'.

Are the legs brought through straight?

No. They are brought through bent, and are straightened at the last moment. This bend-straighten action must be delayed as long as possible.

What is the action of the arms?

Back-up-down. The final sweep-down must be late to match the leg action. Then they must be swung forwards to help you rotate over your heels on landing. ,

Final points?

Remember that accuracy, fast and aggressive running, and a good, hard board-strike are 95% of long jump. Run fast, hold speed and strike hard!

Specimen Programme

Pre-season

DAY I
a: Stretching and low hurdling in gymnasium.
b: 12 × standing triple jump (6 weak leg, 6 strong leg). Measure each jump.
c: Weight training.

DAY II
a: Warm-up.
b: 12 jumps off 9-stride approach, stressing running strongly all the way into the board. Measure each jump.
c: 6 × 150m striding, with complete rest between runs.

DAY III
a: Warm-up.
b: 6 approach-runs over 17 strides, aiming at consistency, without jumping.
c: 300m jog.

In-season

DAY I
a: Warm-up.
b: 12 jumps (9–11-stride approach) stressing take-off 'strike'.
c: 6 × 60m sprint.

DAY II
a: Warm-up.
b: 6 approach-runs over full-distance, without jumping.
c: 3 × 150m fast striding, complete rest between runs.

DAY III
a: Warm-up.
b: 6 full approach-run jumps, stressing 'strike' at take-off. Measure each jump.
c: 6 measured standing triple jumps (3 left foot, 3 right foot).

Long Jump: Boys scoring tables

Amount per extra point	$5\frac{1}{4}''$/0.13m
35 points	21′ 9″ – 6.63
34	21′ 4″ – 6.50
33	20′ 11″ – 6.37
32	20′ 6″ – 6.24
31	20′ 1″ – 6.11
30	19′ 8″ – 5.98
29	19′ 3″ – 5.86
28	18′ 9″ – 5.73
27	18′ 4″ – 5.60
26	17′ 11″ – 5.47
25	17′ 6″ – 5.34
24	17′ 1″ – 5.21
23	16′ 8″ – 5.08
22	16′ 3″ – 4.95
21	15′ 10″ – 4.82
20	15′ 5″ – 4.69
19	14′ 11″ – 4.56
18	14′ 6″ – 4.43
17	14′ 1″ – 4.30
16	13′ 8″ – 4.17
15	13′ 3″ – 4.04
14	12′ 10″ – 3.91
13	12′ 5″ – 3.78
12	12′ 0″ – 3.65
11	11′ 6″ – 3.52
10	11′ 1″ – 3.39
9	10′ 8″ – 3.26
8	10′ 3″ – 3.13
7	9′ 10″ – 3.00
6	9′ 5″ – 2.87
5	9′ 0″ – 2.74
4	8′ 7″ – 2.61
3	8′ 2″ – 2.48
2	7′ 8″ – 2.35
1	7′ 3″ – 2.22

Long jump: Girls scoring tables

Amount per extra point	$3\frac{1}{4}''$/0.08m
35 points	18' 0″ − 5.50
34	17' 9″ − 5.42
33	17' 6″ − 5.34
32	17' 3″ − 5.26
31	17' 0″ − 5.18
30	16' 9″ − 5.10
29	16' 6″ − 5.02
28	16' 3″ − 4.94
27	15' 11″ − 4.86
26	15' 8″ − 4.78
25	15' 5″ − 4.70
24	15' 2″ − 4.62
23	14' 11″ − 4.54
22	14' 8″ − 4.46
21	14' 5″ − 4.38
20	14' 1″ − 4.30
19	13' 9″ − 4.19
18	13' 5″ − 4.08
17	13' 0″ − 3.97
16	12' 8″ − 3.86
15	12' 4″ − 3.75
14	11' 11″ − 3.64
13	11' 7″ − 3.53
12	11' 3″ − 3.42
11	10' 10″ − 3.31
10	10' 6″ − 3.20
9	10' 2″ − 3.09
8	9' 9″ − 2.98
7	9' 5″ − 2.87
6	9' 1″ − 2.76
5	8' 8″ − 2.65
4	8' 4″ − 2.54
3	8' 0″ − 2.43
2	7' 7″ − 2.32
1	7' 3″ − 2.21

A classic hang position

A good high-stepping knee, with the left heel pulled well in. Arms a little wild

Triple Jump

Rules

1. The hop must be made so that the jumper lands first on the foot with which he has taken off. In the step, he lands on the other foot, from which the jump is performed.
2. If the jumper touches the ground with the 'sleeping' leg at any point in the jump then this is counted as a failure.
3. In other respects, the rules relating to long jump apply, in that distances are measured in the same way and the number of attempts allowed is the same.

Most other athletics events seem to me to be either 'natural' activities or sporting versions of warlike activities. Triple jump does not seem to fall into any of these categories.

Few events are really 'natural', but this said, triple jump does not seem to be in line with the other events. It is Celtic in origin, having come from the 19th-century rural sports' activities of Scotland and Ireland. In those times they had a great diversity of hopping and bounding activities but two hops and jump and hop, step and jump were the most popular. Immigrant Scots and Irish carried these events to the United States and the Colonies at the end of the last century, and the first Olympic title was actually won by an Irish-American, Connolly, using two hops and jump. In 1900, it was decided to limit jumpers to hop, step and jump and it has been thus since then, the event now being called 'triple jump'.

I notice there is a rule about the 'sleeping leg'. Why is this?

This rule probably comes from the 19th century when, as I have said, all manner of hopping activities were current. It exists to prevent a jumper dropping his free leg and taking an extra hop from it. This 'trail' of the 'sleeping leg' normally occurs when a jumper is off balance at the end of his hop. He sinks a little in landing and this causes his 'sleeping' leg to scuff the ground.

If I can jump 18′ (5.48m) in the long jump, what distances can I expect to clear after a month's triple jumping?

Double your long jump distance can be achieved fairly quickly, and 39′ (11.89m) – 40′ (12.19m) within a couple of months.

How do I begin?

Mark the ground with some sand about 21′ (6.40m) from the long-jump pit. Off a 3-stride approach, run up and hop, step and jump into the pit. There are only two basics at this point. LAND FLAT-FOOTED and keep the trunk erect.

What happens if I find that I hop, hop and jump or step, step and jump?

This is not uncommon in beginners! Try a standing triple jump from about 16′ from the pit, holding your non-hopping leg behind you. Make it a hop, *drop* and jump, dropping your held leg as you land at the end of the hop. This will make it impossible for you to perform the other variations which you mentioned. When you have mastered the standing triple jump,

Standing triple jump

go back to your 3-stride approach jump. This time, mark the ground at 7′ and 14′.

What is the idea of these marks?

To establish a basic ta-ta-ta rhythm. The big problem in triple jump is the tendency for the jumper to take a massive hop and a short recovery step.

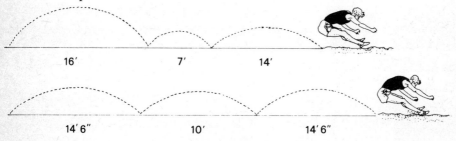

What should I be aiming for, apart from flat-foot landings and an even rhythm?

An upright trunk. Otherwise you will tend to topple at the end of hop and step. Also make sure that you always land in the pit with heels in line.

Why is the approach-run so short?

Because at this point, speed is an enemy. When you have mastered the basics of flat-foot landings and the ta-ta-ta rhythm of triple jump, then you can move up the approach-run distances.

When do I extend the distances between the markers?

As soon as possible! Move them up to 8′ : 8′ : 8′. Naturally, you will find it difficult to reach these markers, and this is where the first major technical point arises. It is the 'drive-out'. Triple jump is a run, followed by a series of 'drive-outs' from one phase to the next.

What does this mean in terms of physical feelings?

Think of the hopping leg driving *backwards* on landing like the threshing paddles of a river-boat. This will cause a *spring* into a long, bounding step. Try this half a dozen times. It is crucial to triple jump.

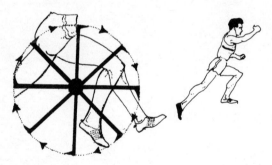

Is there a 'hitch-kick' action in the hop?

Only in that the hopping leg has to pass the non-hopping leg in order that a hop takes place at all! It is, however, essential that there is a good 'split' between the thighs. This helps you to get a good 'drive-out' at the end of the hop.

How else can I increase my step-distance?

By swinging the free leg high into the step on landing from your hop. This gives lift into the step, making it a massive bound.

Should there be the same 'drive-out' from the step?

Yes, though it is best to work on the 'drive-out' from the hop first, as this usually tends to be the weakest in the early stages.

What flight-technique is best for the final jump?

The 'sail' technique

is best for triple jump, as there is little time to execute a 'hang' or a 'hitch-kick'. It is essential that you try to get *up* in this final phase, with a full-blooded leap.

How far am I liable to reach using this even rhythm?

Probably not much above 11′ (3.35m): 11′ (3.35m): 11′ (3.35m). In fact, in your best jumps, the *feeling* will be of a ta-ta-ta rhythm, but the distances may be 17′ (5.18m): 13′ (3.96m): 16′ (4.87m) or 14′ (4.27m): 11′ (3.35m): 14′ (4.27m).

What length of approach-run should I use?

As in long jump, this depends on basic speed. A relatively slow boy of twelve might use only 9 strides, but a fast boy of eighteen might use 19–21 strides. What is essential is that it must be fast and accurate.

How do I achieve accuracy?

By having plenty of run-throughs without jumping, so that you establish a consistent stride-pattern. This can be done as a part of your warm-up.

Are there any other basic points?

Yes. In the step keep the heel of the lead-knee *well in*. A 'poking' action tends to 'brake' you at the end of the step. Also think of churning, driving legs underneath an upright trunk.

When the landing foot is too far in front of body-weight there is a speed loss

Specimen Programme

Pre-season

DAY I
a: Warm-up.
b: Gymnasium. 6 × standing triple jump off both left and right leg. Bounding over low hurdles.
c: 3000m jog, walk, trot.

DAY II
a: Warm-up.
b: 10 triple jumps off 5-stride approach, working on upright trunk and flat-foot landings. Measure each jump.
c: 6 × standing 4 steps and jump. Measure each jump.
d: 3 × 150m stride. Rest between runs.

DAY III
a: Flexibility work.
b: 6 × approach-run practice.
c: 3 × 50m hopping.
d: Weight training.

In-season

DAY I
a: Warm-up.
b: 10 × 9-stride approach triple jumps.
c: 6 × 60m sprinting.

DAY II
a: Warm-up.
b: 6 × approach-run practice.
c: (i) 6 standing triple jumps off strong foot. Measure each jump.
(ii) 6 standing triple jumps off weak foot. Measure each jump.
d: 3 × 140m fast striding.

DAY III
a: Warm-up.
b: 8 × 11-stride approach triple jumps.
c: 6 × 4 steps and jump from a standing start. Measure each jump.
d: Weight training.

Triple Jump: Boys scoring tables

Amount per extra point   9″/0.23m

35 points	44′ 5″ – 13.55
34	43′ 8″ – 13.32
33	42′ 11″ – 13.09
32	42′ 2″ – 12.86
31	41′ 5″ – 12.63
30	40′ 8″ – 12.40
29	39′ 11″ – 12.17
28	39′ 2″ – 11.94
27	38′ 5″ – 11.71
26	37′ 8″ – 11.48
25	36′ 11″ – 11.25
24	36′ 2″ – 11.02
23	35′ 5″ – 10.79
22	34′ 8″ – 10.56
21	33′ 11″ – 10.33
20	33′ 2″ – 10.10
19	32′ 2″ – 9.80
18	31′ 2″ – 9.50
17	30′ 2″ – 9.20
16	29′ 2″ – 8.90
15	28′ 2″ – 8.60
14	27′ 3″ – 8.30
13	26′ 3″ – 8.00
12	25′ 3″ – 7.70
11	24′ 3″ – 7.40
10	23′ 3″ – 7.10
9	22′ 4″ – 6.80
8	21′ 4″ – 6.50
7	20′ 4″ – 6.20
6	19′ 4″ – 5.90
5	18′ 4″ – 5.60
4	17′ 5″ – 5.30
3	16′ 5″ – 5.00
2	15′ 5″ – 4.70
1	14′ 5″ – 4.40

Discus

Decathlete Peter Gabbett lashes out the discus

The discus is thrown from an 8'2½" (2.50m) diameter circle and must be thrown to land within a 45° sector. The thrower must, as in other throwing events from a circle, step out of the circle from its rear half after throwing.

Discus seems to be pretty straightforward as far as rules are concerned.
   Yes. The main problem is to place the discus inside the relatively narrow sector, particularly when you are a beginner.

Was the discus another one of your Scottish events?
   Surprisingly, no! Like javelin, it has its roots in Greece. Unlike javelin, it had no warlike aspects, in that the Greeks did not hurl discoi at their enemies! It is not clear how the ancient Greeks threw the discus and for some time it was thought that they threw from a standing position, from a podium called the 'balbis'. Since the early years of this century, the discus has been thrown from a circle, using a turn.

It is said that discus is the most difficult of the throwing events.

This is to some extent true, in that the discus, like the javelin, presents problems of flighting. If a discus presents too big an angle to air-resistance it will 'die', no matter how powerfully it has been slung.

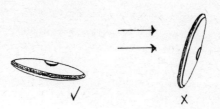

So proper flighting must be learnt from the beginning?

Yes. This means that it is essential to spend some time on hold and spin. The discus is not gripped, but rather held. Note, too, that the wrist is slightly cocked. Try spinning the discus along the ground, off the index-finger, or up into the air.

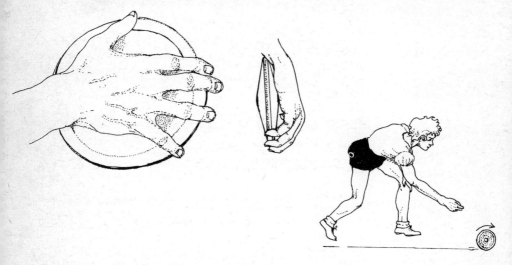

How can this flighting be built into the throw?

A standing throw is best. The discus should be held in the left hand and should be taken back in the right hand in one movement, as you step back on to the toe of the right foot. The discus must be loosely brought back level with the shoulders and slung out from a shallow position, being spun off the index finger.

What about foot-placement?

The feet must be off-set, with left toe in line with right heel, to allow the right hip to be driven forward.

Are there any other points about the standing throw?

Yes. Try to get into a deeper chin–knee–toe position, making sure that you drape a high left arm across your chest. Try to come out of this position by turning the right toe, knee and hip in *hard* to the front.

When I bring back the right foot, should I have the flat of the foot on the ground?

Best to have the toe on the ground, so that it can be driven in quickly.

What about throws using a turn?

If you can throw 100′ from a standing position then you should be able to throw 120′ with a decent turn. What often happens, however, in your early efforts using a turn is that you will only throw about 80′ and that most of your throws will be 'fouls' landing outside the sector.

What type of turn is best to begin with?

The 'I½ turn' in which you stand side-on to the line of throw. This means that you are immediately facing your line of direction. Bring the discus slowly back as in the standing throw and set your left toe along the line of direction. Then simply run across the circle and sling the discus loosely away.

This sounds too easy!

Perhaps! Your natural tendency will be to start by whirling like a dervish and end by slinging a badly-flighted discus out of the throwing sector. You must think of a slow, balanced position at the back of the circle. Think of 'sitting' as you 'set' the left toe in the line of direction.

Why shouldn't I give the discus speed by fast wind-up swings?

Because such fast movements cause tension in the shoulders and will result in the discus 'catching up' at the front of the circle.

What do you mean by 'catching up'?

One of your aims is to gain speed by turning and driving across the circle. Another is to end up in a strongly wound-up throwing position,

with the hips leading the shoulders and the shoulders ahead of the discus. Fast wind-up movements tend to cause the discus to 'catch up' and to result in a rushed throw at the front of the circle.

What about the action of the left arm?

This should be draped across the chest. Think also of looking *over* the left shoulder as you move over the left foot into your turn and of focusing your eyes on a sighting point. This will help your balance.

These movements at the back of the circle seem to be very important.

Crucial. The throw is created at the back of the circle and merely expressed at the front. Your aim must be to sink forward over your left toe, so that you can run across the circle. Here it helps if you hold the right foot on the ground for as long as possible before you go into the turn. This will make it more likely that you have your weight over and beyond your left foot.

What about the 'strike' at the front of the circle?

Think of turning the right toe in as soon as you land at the front of the circle. This will initiate a hard hip-drive. The action is *turn and lift* at the front of the circle. Remember, however, that the discus-arm must be kept flat and long and that the left side should be kept firm.

Is it worth doing the '$1\frac{3}{4}$' turn, facing backwards?

Not in the early stages. You will find that you will be unable to cover the diameter of the circle. More important, turning over the left foot from a back-facing position is more difficult than from a side-on position. If you master the basics of the '$1\frac{1}{2}$' turn, experiment with the '$1\frac{3}{4}$' turn. Illustrated below is a '$1\frac{3}{4}$' turn throw.

Have you any other points?

One. Start slow and finish fast!

Discus Throw: Boys scoring tables

Age group	Under 13 1 kg Under 15 1¼ kg Under 17 1½ kg	Under 20 1¾ kg
Amount per extra point	6′ 6¾″/2m	3′ 3⅜″/1m
35 points		134′ 6″ – 41.00
34		131′ 3″ – 40.00
33		127′ 11″ – 39.00
32	150′ 11″ – 46.00	124′ 8″ – 38.00
31	144′ 4″ – 44.00	121′ 5″ – 37.00
30	137′ 9″ – 42.00	118′ 1″ – 36.00
29	131′ 3″ – 40.00	114′ 10″ – 35.00
28	124′ 8″ – 38.00	111′ 6″ – 34.00
27	118′ 1″ – 36.00	108′ 3″ – 33.00
26	111′ 6″ – 34.00	105′ 0″ – 32.00
25	105′ 0″ – 32.00	101′ 8″ – 31.00
24	101′ 8″ – 31.00	98′ 5″ – 30.00
23	98′ 5″ – 30.00	95′ 2″ – 29.00
22	95′ 2″ – 29.00	91′ 10″ – 28.00
21	91′ 10″ – 28.00	88′ 7″ – 27.00
20	88′ 7″ – 27.00	85′ 4″ – 26.00
19	85′ 4″ – 26.00	82′ 0″ – 25.00
18	82′ 0″ – 25.00	78′ 9″ – 24.00
17	78′ 9″ – 24.00	75′ 5″ – 23.00
16	75′ 5″ – 23.00	72′ 2″ – 22.00
15	72′ 2″ – 22.00	68′ 11″ – 21.00
14	68′ 11″ – 21.00	65′ 7″ – 20.00
13	65′ 7″ – 20.00	62′ 4″ – 19.00
12	62′ 4″ – 19.00	59′ 1″ – 18.00
11	59′ 1″ – 18.00	57′ 5″ – 17.50
10	55′ 9″ – 17.00	55′ 9″ – 17.00
9	52′ 6″ – 16.00	54′ 1″ – 16.50
8	49′ 2″ – 15.00	52′ 6″ – 16.00
7	45′ 11″ – 14.00	50′ 10″ – 15.50
6	42′ 8″ – 13.00	49′ 2″ – 15.00
5	39′ 4″ – 12.00	47′ 7″ – 14.50
4	36′ 1″ – 11.00	45′ 11″ – 14.00
3	32′ 10″ – 10.00	44′ 3″ – 13.50
2	29′ 6″ – 9.00	42′ 8″ – 13.00
1	26′ 3″ – 8.00	41′ 0″ – 12.50

SAFETY, relating to the throwing events, should be observed at All times.

Old-weight Implement Adjustments

<small>DISCUS</small>

If the new categories of throwing implements are not available, then the following adjustments should be made. Read off the number of points gained and then take off the following number of points to obtain the final correct score.

                                    Points Down

Under 15 Boys Discus
1 kg (instead of $1\frac{1}{4}$ kg)   4
Under 17 Boys Discus
1 kg (instead of $1\frac{1}{2}$ kg)   9
Under 20 Boys Discus
$1\frac{1}{2}$ kg (instead of $1\frac{3}{4}$ kg)   4

Discus Throw: Girls scoring tables

Amount per extra point	1 kg 2' 5½"/0.75m
35 points	110' 9" − 33.75
34	108' 3" − 33.00
33	105' 10" − 32.25
32	103' 4" − 31.50
31	100' 11" − 30.75
30	98' 5". − 30.00
29	96' 0" − 29.25
28	93' 6" − 28.50
27	91' 1" − 27.75
26	88' 7" − 27.00
25	86' 2" − 26.25
24	83' 8" − 25.50
23	81' 3" − 24.75
22	78' 9" − 24.00
21	76' 4" − 23.25
20	73' 10" − 22.50
19	70' 11" − 21.60
18	67' 11" − 20.70
17	65' 0" − 19.80
16	62' 0" − 18.90
15	59' 1" − 18.00
14	56' 1" − 17.10
13	53' 2" − 16.20
12	50' 3" − 15.30
11	47' 3" − 14.40
10	44' 4" − 13.50
9	41' 4" − 12.60
8	38' 5" − 11.70
7	35' 5" − 10.80
6	32' 6" − 9.90
5	29' 7" − 9.00
4	26' 7" − 8.10
3	23' 8" − 7.20
2	20' 8" − 6.30
1	17' 9" − 5.40

Shot Put

The shot is putted, rather than thrown. This means that the shot must touch or be in close proximity to the chin and that the hand shall not be dropped below this position during each put.

The put takes place from within a 7′ (2.13m) diameter circle and the shot has to land within a 65° sector. A 'foul' occurs if the putter:

1. Steps out of the front of the circle during or after the put.
2. Places any part of his body on the *top* of the stop-board.
3. Touches any ground outside the rim of the circle.

What is the significance of keeping the shot 'in close proximity to the neck'?

This is to prevent throwing. This problem hardly exists with the heavier shots, but in the early stages of putting when a small, relatively light shot is used, many young athletes do have a tendency to pull the shot behind the line of the shoulder. To save problems, *pin the shot into the neck* until you strike it at the front of the circle.

If the shot has landed, can I then step out of the front half of the circle?

No. This would be a 'foul'. You must step out of the back half of the circle.

Am I allowed to touch the stop-board at all?

Yes. You *are* allowed to touch the *inside* of the stop-board. The *top* of the stop-board is, however, not part of the throwing area and must not be touched.

How did the event come into the athletics programme?

Like many throwing events, it is of Scottish origin, having originated in the Scottish Highlands, probably in the 14th century. The 'shot' was originally a stone and it was only in the middle of the 19th century that cannon-shot began to be used.

How should I begin?

At first a standing put is best, to give you a 'feel' for the event and to establish one or two basic points.

How do I grip the shot?

The shot is not 'gripped'. It is propped in the fingers with the thumb and little finger supporting the shot and the three other fingers behind it. I call this 'two for balance and three for power'.

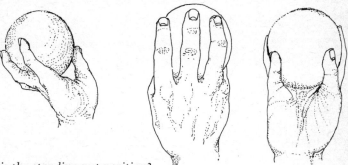

What is the standing put position?

Face the front, right elbow well out, feet hip-width apart and left arm high. Put the shot first *without bending the knees*. Mark the distance you have reached.

What are the essentials at this point?

Keep the 'transmission point' fixed. This means keeping the right elbow fixed in position throughout the throw and keeping the left arm high.

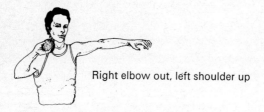

Right elbow out, left shoulder up

Next, try to 'chase' the shot out as far as possible with your elbow and hand. This should result in an improved distance, which you should mark with your peg.

What is the point of this 'chasing'?

To increase the *range* of your put. This is basic to all good putting. Our next step, to twist the trunk further back, further increases this range. Pull the shot as far round as you can and put.

When can I use my legs?

As soon as possible! The only reason for these short-range puts is to limit the number of possible errors and to establish certain basics with the minimum of side-issues. Now bend the knees. Think of *lift and chase*!

How important is this leg-drive?

Vital! The legs contain the strongest muscles in the body. Strangely, most novices try to 'strike' the shot with some of the *weakest* muscles, the muscles of the arms. The big distance-improvement when you use your legs will show you how important this leg-drive is. Think of *lifting the right hip* viciously up and over the stop-board.

Mexico City 1968. The massive Randy Matson gets ready to explode from a powerful putting position

Should I try to increase trunk-twist?

Yes. This will again increase range and put-distance.

When should I move on to the normal standing put position?

When you feel that you have grooved in the idea of 'lift and chase' and of keeping putting arm and left arm positions steady.

What are the main points in this type of put?

First, make sure the feet are slightly off-set. The right heel should be in line with the left toe. This makes it possible for the right hip to be driven up and over the top of the stop-board. Next, try to get the toe, knee and shot in line, keeping the back flat. The right foot should be parallel to the centre line. Remember that putting is not a series of static positions, but a series of positions from which you flow explosively.

Once I have the correct positions, what should I try to do?

Think of driving the right hip up into the throw, keeping the shot pinned into the neck until the last moment.

Should I revise the 'chasing'?

Yes. All of the points so far have been a re-stressing of points already raised. Think again of 'lift and chase'.

What about movement across the circle?

This gives the shot greater velocity and you do not have to wait until you have mastered every aspect of the standing put before you move on to some type of 'shift' across the circle. A simple, primitive method is the cross-step—a 'right over left foot' action.

What are the points to consider?

Think of *keeping the shot moving*! When the right foot lands at the front of the circle, keep the shot moving forward. Any checking will lose you much of the advantage of your 'shift'.

Have you any other points?

Again, drive the right hip up hard and chase that ball out with your finger-tips.

What other methods are there of 'shift'?

Here is a simple 'side-on' technique. It is important here to establish a simple rhythm at the back of the circle. This is dictated by the action of the left leg. Its action is up, in and out. It is up as the trunk lays back, in as the right leg flexes and out as the right leg drives across the circle.

Is the movement across the circle a hop?

No. It is a 'shift' in which the right foot skims the ground. This means that it is easier to maintain forward speed.

What happens when the right foot lands at the front of the circle?

Exactly the same as in the cross-step technique. The only other problem in this technique is the tendency for the trunk to straighten up as you cross the circle, giving you a weak, shallow position. You must try to stay back over your right foot.

What about other advanced techniques?

There is the O'Brien technique. This involves facing backwards, and deeper positions at the front of the circle. These two factors present difficulties for the novice who finds it easier if he can see exactly where he is going and has to handle only shallow positions at the front of the circle.

Do I come off the right toe at the back of the circle, using the O'Brien technique?

No. From the heel. If you 'settle' properly as the left leg comes in to meet the right and drive the left thigh towards the stop-board, you will come correctly off the right heel. The basic rhythm is: left foot, left knee in, left thigh out.

Should the left and right feet land at the same time at the front of the circle?

There should be as little delay as possible between the landing of the right and left feet. To this end, the left foot should be low as you shift across the circle. If there is a delay, then the body will straighten up and you will lose the deep putting position which you seek.

Should the left leg shoot straight back towards the stop-board?

It should *feel* as if it is shooting straight back. In fact, if the feet are to be off-set at the front, the left foot must always be slightly to the left when it lands.

What should be the position of the right foot at the centre of the circle?

Parallel to centre line, underneath the shot. Most important, the hip must be kept in. Any 'sitting' will make it difficult to get an effective leg-drive.

OFF   IN   OUT

O'Brien technique

Mike Winch showing the power essential for top shot-putting

Is the right leg-action the same as in the side-on put?
    Yes. Think of driving the right side hard against a firm left leg. Keep pressing up over the stop board.

Have you any final points?
    Keeping the shot moving is crucial. Keep your transmission points fixed. Shot put is an explosive event. Hit that shot hard!

Shot Put: Boys scoring tables

Age group	
	Under 13 6 lb
	Under 14 7 lb
	Under 15 4 kg
	Under 17 5 kg
	Under 20 6¼ kg
Amount per extra point	11″/0.27m

35 points	43′ 4″	– 13.20
34	42′ 5″	– 12.93
33	41′ 7″	– 12.66
32	40′ 8″	– 12.39
31	39′ 9″	– 12.12
30	38′ 11″	– 11.85
29	38′ 0″	– 11.58
28	37′ 1″	– 11.31
27	36′ 3″	– 11.04
26	35′ 4″	– 10.77
25	34′ 6″	– 10.50
24	33′ 7″	– 10.23
23	32′ 8″	– 9.96
22	31′ 10″	– 9.69
21	30′ 11″	– 9.42
20	30′ 0″	– 9.15
19	28′ 11″	– 8.80
18	27′ 9″	– 8.45
17	26′ 7″	– 8.10
16	25′ 5″	– 7.75
15	24′ 4″	– 7.40
14	23′ 6″	– 7.15
13	22′ 4″	– 6.80
12	21′ 8″	– 6.60
11	21′ 0″	– 6.40
10	20′ 4″	– 6.20
9	19′ 8″	– 6.00
8	19′ 1″	– 5.80
7	18′ 5″	– 5.60
6	17′ 9″	– 5.40
5	17′ 1″	– 5.20
4	16′ 5″	– 5.00
3	15′ 9″	– 4.80
2	15′ 1″	– 4.60
1	14′ 5″	– 4.40

SAFETY, relating to the throwing events, should be observed at All times.

Old-weight Implement Adjustments

SHOT PUT

If the new categories of throwing implements are not available, then the following adjustments should be made. Read off the number of points gained and then take off the following number of points to obtain the final correct score.

Points Down

Under 17 Boys Shot 10 lb
(instead of 5 kg/11 lb)   4
Under 20 Boys Shot 12 lb
(instead of 6¼ kg/13¾ lb)   4
Under 15 Girls Shot 7 lb
(instead of 3¼ kg/7¼ lb)   Same

Shot put: Girls scoring tables

Age group	Under 13 6 lb Under 15 3¼ kg Under 20 4 kg
Amount per extra point	4¾″/0.12m
35 points	33′ 0″ – 10.05
34	32′ 7″ – 9.93
33	32′ 2″ – 9.81
32	31′ 10″ – 9.69
31	31′ 5″ – 9.57
30	31′ 0″ – 9.45
29	30′ 8″ – 9.33
28	30′ 3″ – 9.21
27	29′ 10″ – 9.09
26	29′ 5″ – 8.97
25	29′ 1″ – 8.85
24	28′ 8″ – 8.73
23	28′ 3″ – 8.61
22	27′ 10″ – 8.49
21	27′ 6″ – 8.37
20	27′ 1″ – 8.25
19	26′ 3″ – 8.00
18	25′ 5″ – 7.75
17	24′ 7″ – 7.50
16	23′ 10″ – 7.25
15	23′ 0″ – 7.00
14	22′ 2″ – 6.75
13	21′ 4″ – 6.50
12	20′ 6″ – 6.25
11	19′ 8″ – 6.00
10	18′ 10″ – 5.75
9	18′ 1″ – 5.50
8	17′ 3″ – 5.25
7	16′ 5″ – 5.00
6	15′ 7″ – 4.75
5	14′ 9″ – 4.50
4	13′ 11″ – 4.25
3	13′ 2″ – 4.00
2	12′ 4″ – 3.75
1	11′ 6″ – 3.50

David Travis prepares to unleash from a strong position

Javelin

The javelin has to land within a specific area and must land point-first. The javelin *must* be held at the binding and the thrower must not during the throw make any attempt to turn completely around. As in other throws, the thrower must not cross the throwing arc after release and must retreat back along the run-way. The area to the side of the run-way must not be encroached upon after the throw.

What is the reason for the rule about not turning 'completely around'?
    Back in 1956, some Spanish athletes, using the technique of a local bar-throwing event, started to turn with the javelin and hurled it prodigious distances. Within months, other athletes had copied this technique and an Italian discus-thrower, Consolini, was rumoured to have thrown 320' (97.53m)! One problem with this technique was that

throwers, who soaped the javelin to make it easier to throw, had
difficulty in predicting exactly where the javelin was going to land. There
was therefore a danger that, at major meetings, javelin might well
become a blood-sport! Another problem was that stadia were going
to become too small for throws of these lengths. This technique was
therefore banned almost immediately.

Does the javelin have actually to stick in the ground?
    No. It is only required to strike ground *point-first*. If it lands at a
shallow angle or on hard ground, it is unlikely to actually stick in the
ground.

How did the javelin event come into existence?
    It comes directly from the ancient Olympics, where it originally
occurred only in the pentathlon event. It was one of the first throwing
events to be introduced when the Olympics were revived in 1896.

What are the basics?
    First, a good grip. You must have the javelin lying *along* the palm,
using the palm as a platform. Next, place the index-finger and third-finger
behind the binding. This is the 'claw' grip, a simple, powerful hold
on the spear.

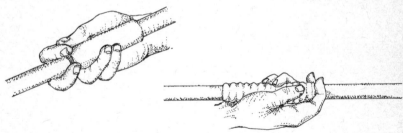

What next?
    Place a marker ten to fifteen feet away. Draw the javelin well back,
close to the face, point down and *stab it* viciously at your marker. Think
of pulling hard *through* the javelin.

Surely javelin is not an accuracy event. What about distance-throwing?

The idea of the stabbing practice is to help you gain experience of grip and straight-line pull in a simple 'fun' situation. Still, as you say, the event is not for accuracy. Try a standing throw. Keep a flat, high javelin and lean back.

Step forward on to the left foot and pull straight through the javelin, right over your left foot.

What are the points to note?

You must keep the javelin flat and close to the face, and you must at all times keep it steady. Drive the right hip and shoulder in hard.

What about a running throw?

It is best to do plenty of standing throws to get the 'feel' of the javelin, but naturally you will want to throw from a run. Try this from 3–5 strides. The basic points are:

1. Reach well back with the hand *up and back* as you go into your run.
2. Keep your hips to the front.
3. Keep the javelin flat and steady.
4. Whisper a stride-count as you run. One - two - three - four - THROW!

Have you any other points?

Try to keep the throw *fluent*, building speed from first to last strides. Start slow and finish fast is the best advice. Also, keep the arm loose and whippy.

What about full-length approach-runs?

Speed is an enemy in the early stages. Controlled throws off a short run are best, because you are then able to get the 'feel' of long, fluent pulling positions. However, in a full approach-run of ten strides the first five strides are for acceleration, the next three for withdrawal of the javelin and the last two for getting into and through a throwing position.

I see that the throw takes place some distance before the line. Doesn't this mean a loss of distance?

No. Javelin-throwing takes place at much higher horizontal speeds than the other throws and you therefore need space for recovery. If you threw from the arc-line itself you would be likely to topple beyond it and thus 'foul'.

Should I go back to counting aloud as I run?

Yes, many throwers do this. It helps to maintain rhythm. Think in terms of building speed all the way into release. *Hurl yourself* after the javelin at release!

What about cross-steps?

These are the steps immediately before throwing, when you try to get into a strong throwing position over a bent right knee. Think of getting high knees as you hit your check-mark two strides out.

You say two strides out. Does this mean that I need a long approach-run, say seven strides?

Yes, otherwise you will be trying to get into a 'lay back' position almost immediately.

Could you summarise the basic points?

1. 'Claw' grip, palm up.
2. Long, relaxed arm.
3. Flat javelin, close to head.
4. Hips to the front.
5. Sweep the right foot ahead as you go into the cross-step.
6. Right heel down stride as you land for the cross-step.
7. Drive the right hip hard in ahead of a high flailing right shoulder and hit the javelin *viciously*, pulling all the way over the left foot.

That is a fair amount to remember.

Yes, but as in the other events, you must only work on one point at a time. For instance, you might spend your warm-up throws on 'stabbing' stressing a loose arm and palm up. Then your next throws might stress a flat, steady javelin and hips to the front, off a short run.

Javelin Throw: Boys scoring tables

Age group	*Under 15* 600 gm *Under 17* 700 gm *Under 20* 800 gm
Amount per extra point	5' 3"/1.60m
35 points	173' 11" − 53.00
34	168' 8" − 51.40
33	163' 5" − 49.80
32	158' 2" − 48.20
31	152' 11" − 46.60
30	147' 8" − 45.00
29	142' 5" − 43.40
28	137' 2" − 41.80
27	131' 11"− 40.20
26	126' 8" − 38.60
25	121' 5" − 37.00
24	116' 2" − 35.40
23	110' 11"− 33.80
22	105' 8" − 32.20
21	100' 5" − 30.60
20	95' 2" − 29.00
19	89' 11"− 27.40
18	85' 4" − 26.00
17	82' 0" − 25.00
16	78' 9" − 24.00
15	75' 5" − 23.00
14	72' 2" − 22.00
13	68' 11"− 21.00
12	65' 7" − 20.00
11	62' 4" − 19.00
10	59' 1" − 18.00
9	55' 9" − 17.00
8	52' 6" − 16.00
7	49' 2" − 15.00
6	45' 11"− 14.00
5	42' 8" − 13.00
4	39' 4" − 12.00
3	36' 1" − 11.00
2	32' 10"− 10.00
1	29' 6" − 9.00

SAFETY, relating to the throwing events, should be observed at All times.

Javelin Throw: Girls scoring tables

Amount per extra point	600 gm 2' 8½"/0.825m
35 points	114' 10" – 35.00
34	112' 2" – 34.17
33	109' 5" – 33.35
32	106' 8" – 32.52
31	104' 0" – 31.70
30	101' 1" – 30.82
29	98' 5" – 30.00
28	95' 9" – 29.17
27	93' 0" – 28.35
26	90' 4" – 27.52
25	87' 7" – 26.70
24	84' 9" – 25.82
23	82' 0" – 25.00
22	79' 4" – 24.17
21	76' 7" – 23.35
20	73' 11" – 22.52
19	71' 1" – 21.65
18	68' 3" – 20.80
17	65' 6" – 19.95
16	62' 8" – 19.10
15	59' 11" – 18.25
14	57' 1" – 17.40
13	54' 4" – 16.55
12	51' 6" – 15.70
11	48' 9" – 14.85
10	45' 11" – 14.00
9	43' 2" – 13.15
8	40' 4" – 12.30
7	37' 7" – 11.45
6	34' 10" – 10.60
5	32' 0" – 9.75
4	29' 3" – 8.90
3	26' 5" – 8.05
2	23' 8" – 7.20
1	20' 10" – 6.35

Hammer

The hammer is thrown from a 7' diameter circle, the hammer having to land within a 45° sector. As in other throws from a circle, the thrower must retreat from the rear half of the circle after throwing. Once the thrower has started his preliminary swings and turns, he cannot stop and recommence his throw if the hammer-head has touched ground. It should, however, be noted that the hammer-head can be placed outside the circle before the thrower starts his preliminary swings.

The only rule which is not completely clear to me is the one about restarting the throw after the hammer-head has touched the ground.

This *is* a tough one! If at any point (even in your preliminary swings) you stop and allow the hammer-head to touch the ground, then this is a 'foul'. If, however, you stop and restart the throw without allowing the nammer-head to touch ground then it is a fair throw.

The biggest problem in schools is the lack of throwing nets and the damage to grounds which hammers cause. Is there any way round this?

There is, but it is rarely in the hands of pupils. Almost any physical education teacher who wants to develop hammer as a school event can do something about it. Sandbag and chain-head hammers reduce ground damage to negligible proportions. Safe nets can be constructed for as little as £30 by the school itself.

What about ground damage?

Many schools have odd areas of little-used ground on which hard-head hammers can be thrown. Initially, these areas may only allow throws in the 120' region, but this is enough for a beginning. Nevertheless, I must admit that this is one event in which young athletes can come up against what appear to be insurmountable obstacles. No boy can start hammer-throwing without the necessary equipment and this is dependent on the approval of his physical education master.

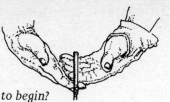
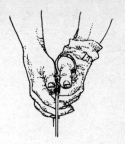

How is it best to begin?
First, the hold. Left hand inside the right.

Is a left-hand glove necessary?
Initially no, but once you start to release the hammer at higher speeds you will find the handle pulling on your left hand, so it is best to wear an old leather glove.

Any other equipment points?
If possible, it is best to start on a short-wire hammer, in the 3′ (91cm) to 3′6″ (1.06m) region. This can be made of nylon cord.

What is the reason for this short wire?
Most beginners find it difficult to handle the standard 4′ (1.21m) wire. I know *I* did! The shorter wire makes the hammer easier to control.

What is the best footwear?
Ordinary plimsolls will do. If, however, you become a real hammer fanatic, then you will want to buy a special hammer-shoe for your left foot.

Have you any other points?
Yes. Safety is vital, so you must never throw if there are people around or in front of you. There must never be any 'throwing back' to friends.

What are the first technical points?
To begin with, have a throw! Stand at the front of the circle with your back to the line of throw, give the hammer a couple of preliminary swings and let fly!

A standing throw

Surely the hammer is a turning event?

Yes, but the idea of these standing throws is to give you a 'feel' of the implement and an experience of hurling it in a simple situation.

How do I learn to turn?

'Stutter' turns are a good way to get the 'feel' of turning, but first it is worthwhile to get some idea of the preliminary swings. Place the hammer behind your right foot on full stretch and lift it up in front, brushing your forehead with the back of the right hand. As the hammer drops to its low point straighten the arms.

Think of 'high' (arms bent) low (arms straight). Think of the hammer swinging in a wide loose arc.

Should the legs be straight?

The legs should be bent with feet a little beyond hip-width apart. You should move your weight freely from foot to foot as you swing the hammer. Remember that the hammer-swings start in the feet.

So much for the preliminary swings. How do I perform these 'stutter' turns?

On your second swing, let the hammer fly well out in front with long loose arms and start to make tiny stuttering steps along a straight line. Look at the hammer-head. This will help your balance.

How many turns should I take?

Turn until you feel that you are beginning to lose your ability to turn in a straight line. Think of keeping the arms straight during your turns and of 'sitting away' from the hammer. With a short-wire hammer the pull on your arms and shoulders should not be too great.

How do these stutter turns relate to proper turns?
    A great deal. If you can give the hammer two loose, rangy, preliminary swings and turn in a straight line with straight arms and bent knees, then you have most of the basic elements of the normal throw from a turn.

How do I begin on these turns?
    Turning is done on the heel of the left and the toe of the right foot.

This is the reason for the words 'heel-toe' in describing the turns. Try a few of these without the hammer to a one/two rhythm. 'One' is the turning on the left heel and the pointing of the left toe in the line of direction. 'Two' is the picking up of the right foot, close to the left as the left continues its turn. This means that you are now in the same position as that in which you started.

What are the basics in the turns with the hammer?
    I suggest first a one-turn throw, using a short-handled hammer. Make two preliminary swings, making sure that the hammer is high on the left and low on the right. On the second swing, let the hammer well out and turn on the heel as the hammer passes in front of you. This brings you into the delivery position, from which you simply let the hammer flail out, with long straight arms.

Is this one-turn throw a good lead-in to two- and three-turn throws?
    Only up to a point. From one turn you can always manage some sort of delivery, even if you are off balance. This is the limitation of one-turn throwing. You must therefore move on to two-turn throwing as soon as possible.

What must I aim for in these throws?
    First, easy swings. Next, sweeping the hammer out with straight arms as you go into the first turn. Last, keep the weight well over the left heel all through the throw. Think in terms of pinning the left heel down.

Are there any other points?
    Keep a 'sitting' position throughout the throw with a straight back. Never sacrifice control for speed. Three smooth, fluent turns with straight arms will send the hammer a long way. Remember that the feet are the masters of the throw.

Starting position

2nd wind-up swing

1st turn

2nd turn

3rd turn

Delivery

Old-weight Implement Adjustments

If the new categories of throwing implements are not available, then the following adjustments should be made. Read off the number of points gained and then take off the following number of points to obtain the final correct score.

	Points Down
Under 17 Boys Hammer 10 lb (instead of 5 kg/11 lb)	3
Under 20 Boys Hammer 12 lb (instead of $6\frac{1}{4}$ kg/$13\frac{3}{4}$ lb)	5

Delivery!

Hammer Throw: Boys scoring tables

Age group	Under 14 6 lb Under 15 4 kg Under 17 5 kg Under 20 6¼ kg
Amount per extra point	3′ 11¼″/1.20m
35 points	148′ 3″ − 45.20
34	144′ 4″ − 44.00
33	140′ 5″ − 42.80
32	136′ 6″ − 41.60
31	132′ 6″ − 40.40
30	128′ 7″ − 39.20
29	124′ 8″ − 38.00
28	120′ 9″ − 36.80
27	116′ 9″ − 35.60
26	112′ 10″ − 34.40
25	108′ 11″ − 33.20
24	105′ 0″ − 32.00
23	101′ 0″ − 30.80
22	97′ 1″ − 29.60
21	93′ 2″ − 28.40
20	89′ 3″ − 27.20
19	85′ 4″ − 26.00
18	81′ 4″ − 24.80
17	77′ 5″ − 23.60
16	73′ 6″ − 22.40
15	69′ 7″ − 21.20
14	65′ 7″ − 20.00
13	61′ 8″ − 18.80
12	57′ 9″ − 17.60
11	53′ 10″− 16.40
10	49′ 10″− 15.20
9	45′ 11″ − 14.00
8	42′ 0″ − 12.80
7	39′ 4″ − 12.00
6	37′ 9″ − 11.50
5	36′ 1″ − 11.00
4	34′ 5″ − 10.50
3	32′ 10″− 10.00
2	31′ 2″ − 9.50
1	29′ 6″ − 9.00

SAFETY, relating to the throwing events, should be observed at All times.

Throwing the Cricket Ball:
Boys scoring tables

Age group	*Under 13* 4¾ oz
Amount per extra point	7′ 4½″/2.25m
35 points	−
34	−
33	−
32	−
31	−
30	−
29	−
28	−
27	−
26	−
25	223′ 11″ − 68.25
24	216′ 6″ − 66.00
23	209′ 2″ − 63.75
22	201′ 9″ − 61.50
21	194′ 4″ − 59.25
20	187′ 0″ − 57.00
19	179′ 7″ − 54.75
18	172′ 3″ − 52.50
17	164′ 10″ − 50.25
16	157′ 6″ − 48.00
15	150′ 1″ − 45.75
14	142′ 8″ − 43.50
13	135′ 4″ − 41.25
12	128′ 0″ − 39.00
11	120′ 7″ − 36.75
10	113′ 2″ − 34.50
9	105′ 9″ − 32.25
8	98′ 5″ − 30.00
7	91′ 0″ − 27.75
6	83′ 8″ − 25.50
5	76′ 3″ − 23.25
4	68′ 11″ − 21.00
3	61′ 6″ − 18.75
2	54′ 2″ − 16.50
1	46′ 9″ − 14.25

Throwing the Rounders Ball: Girls scoring tables

Age group	Under 14
Amount per extra point	5′ 1″/1.55m
35 points	–
34	–
33	–
32	–
31	–
30	–
29	–
28	–
27	–
26	–
25	162′ 5″ – 49.50
24	157′ 6″ – 48.00
23	152′ 7″ – 46.50
22	147′ 8″ – 45.00
21	142′ 8″ – 43.50
20	137′ 9″ – 42.00
19	132′ 10″ – 40.50
18	127′ 11″ – 39.00
17	123′ 0″ – 37.50
16	118′ 1″ – 36.00
15	113′ 2″ – 34.50
14	108′ 3″ – 33.00
13	103′ 4″ – 31.50
12	98′ 5″ – 30.00
11	93′ 6″ – 28.50
10	88′ 7″ – 27.00
9	83′ 8″ – 25.50
8	78′ 9″ – 24.00
7	73′ 10″ – 22.50
6	68′ 0″ – 20.75
5	62′ 4″ – 19.00
4	56′ 7″ – 17.25
3	50′ 10″ – 15.50
2	45′ 1″ – 13.75
1	39′ 4″ – 12.00

SAFETY, relating to the throwing events, should be observed at All times.